Traditional

Chicago

Cookbook

Introduction

Chicago, Illinois is located on the north east part of the United States on the shores of Lake Michigan, which is one of the five Great Lakes of North America.

Chicago has a large number of regional specialties that reflect the city's ethnic and working-class roots. These include the Chicago Deep Dish Pizza, the Chicago Style Hot Dog and the Italian Beef sandwich.

There are many famous people from Chicago including Harrison Ford, Tina Fey and John Malkovich.

Chicago is the setting for many books, movies and television shows including the medical drama E.R., the movie Risky Business and the Divergent trilogy by Veronica Roth.

Chicago has a long history of craft brewing. There are many micro breweries, brew pubs and regional brewers.

The cultural diversity of the city has led to many Chicago specialty dishes with ethnic influences including Mexican, Greek, Italian, Polish and Chinese.

I have put together a cookbook with some of the best and most well-known recipes from Chicago that best represent the spirit of the Windy City. Enjoy!

Chicago Dip

Ingredients:

1 (10 oz.) package frozen chopped spinach, thawed and drained
1 cup sour cream
1 cup mayonnaise
3/4 cup chopped green onions
2 tsps. dried parsley
1 tsp. lemon juice
1/2 tsp. seasoned salt
1 (1 lb.) loaf round, crusty Italian bread

Directions:

1. In a large mixing bowl, combine spinach, sour cream, mayonnaise, green onions, parsley, lemon juice, and salt.
2. Mix until well blended, then refrigerate.
3. Cut a circle out of the top of the bread and scoop out the inside.
4. Tear the inside into pieces for dipping.
5. Spoon the dip into the center of the bread bowl and serve accompanied by the pieces of bread for dipping.
6. Preheat oven to 300 degrees F (150 degrees C).
7. Serve and enjoy!

Chicago Deep Dish Pizza Dip

Ingredients:

1 (1.37 oz.) package spaghetti sauce mix
1 cup part-skim ricotta cheese
1 egg
2 cups shredded mozzarella cheese, divided
1/2 cup grated parmesan cheese
1/4 cup mini pepperoni slices or chopped pepperoni

Directions:

1. Preheat oven to 375 degrees F. Prepare sauce as directed on package. Cool slightly.
2. Mix ricotta cheese, egg, 1 cup of the mozzarella cheese and Parmesan cheese in large bowl.
3. Spread in 9-inch round cake pan sprayed with no stick cooking spray. Top with prepared Spaghetti Sauce.
4. Sprinkle with remaining 1 cup mozzarella cheese and pepperoni.
5. Bake 20 minutes or until heated through. Serve with sliced garlic bread, breadsticks or toasted baguette slices.

Chicago Red Hot (Chicago Style Hot Dog)

The hot dog is topped with yellow mustard, chopped white onions, bright green sweet pickle relish, a dill pickle spear, tomato slices or wedges, pickled sport peppers and a dash of celery salt. Notice the absence of ketchup.

The complete assembly of a Chicago hot dog is said to be "dragged through the garden" due to the many toppings.

The method for cooking the hot dog itself varies depending on the vendor's preference. Most often they are steamed, water-simmered, or less often grilled over charcoal (in which case they are referred to as "char-dogs").

The canonical recipe does not include ketchup, and there is a widely shared, strong opinion among many Chicagoans and aficionados that ketchup is unacceptable.

A number of Chicago hot dog vendors do not offer ketchup as a condiment.

Ingredients:

1 all-beef hot dog
1 poppy seed hot dog bun
1 tbsp. yellow mustard
1 tbsp. sweet green pickle relish
1 tbsp. chopped onion
4 tomato wedges
1 dill pickle spear
2 sport peppers 1 dash celery salt

Directions:

1. Bring a pot of water to a boil.
2. Reduce heat to low, place hot dog in water, and cook 5 minutes or until done.
3. Remove hot dog and set aside.
4. Carefully place a steamer basket into the pot and steam the hot dog bun 2 minutes or until warm.

5. Place hot dog in the steamed bun. Pile on the toppings in this order: yellow mustard, sweet green pickle relish, onion, tomato wedges, pickle spear, sport peppers, and celery salt. The tomatoes should be nestled between the hot dog and the top of the bun.
6. Place the pickle between the hot dog and the bottom of the bun. Don't even think about ketchup!
7. Serve and enjoy!

Chicago Style Roast Duck

Ingredients:

1 (4 lb.) whole duck
1 tbsp. garlic powder
1 tbsp. onion powder salt and pepper, to taste
2 tbsps. caraway seeds

Directions:

1. Preheat oven to 425 degrees F (220 degrees C).
2. Wash duck and pat dry. Score breast and legs by cutting into skin with sharp knife, going 2/3 of the way through the skin, being careful not to slice into meat.
3. Season the cavity and the outside of the duck with garlic powder, onion powder, salt, and pepper; massage spices into meat.
4. Sprinkle caraway seeds over duck, and into scored skin.
5. Place on a rack in a roasting pan, breast side up.
6. Roast duck in preheated oven for 15 minutes. Turn breast side down, and roast for an additional 15 minutes.
7. Remove duck from the oven; reduce oven temperature to 350 degrees F. Turn duck breast side up again, and return to the oven for 20 minutes. Turn duck one more time, breast side down. Roast for a final 20 minutes.
8. Remove duck from oven and allow to rest for 10 minutes before serving.
9. Serve and enjoy!

Chicago Stuffed Pizza

Ingredients:

2 tsps. white sugar
1 cup warm water (110 degrees F/45 degrees C)
1 tsp. active dry yeast
3 cups unbleached all-purpose flour, divided
1/2 cup warm water (110 degrees F/45 degrees C)
1/2 cup yellow cornmeal
1 1/2 tsps. salt
2 tbsps. olive oil
1/4 lb. spicy Italian sausage - browned, drained and crumbled
9 oz. shredded mozzarella cheese
1/4 cup grated Parmesan cheese
1/3 cup diced pepperoni
1/4 cup chopped onion
1/8 cup chopped green bell pepper
1 tsp. dried oregano
3 cloves garlic, sliced
1/2 cup tomato sauce

Directions:

1. To Make Dough: In a small bowl, dissolve sugar in 1 cup warm water; in a separate small bowl combine the yeast, 1/2 cup flour, and 1/2 cup warm water.
2. Mix together and let rest in bowl for about 20 minutes, until foamy.
3. Meanwhile, in a medium bowl mix together remaining 2 1/2 cups flour with cornmeal and salt; remove half of this mixture from bowl and stir 1 cup sugar water into bowl.
4. When well mixed, return second half of flour/cornmeal mixture to bowl and mix all together; then stir in yeast mixture.
5. Knead dough on a lightly floured surface until smooth and elastic, about 8 to 12 minutes.
6. Place dough in a lightly oiled bowl and cover with plastic wrap. Let rise until doubled in volume.
7. Preheat oven to 450 degrees F (230 degrees C).

Stuffing Directions:

1. In a large bowl combine the sausage, mozzarella cheese, Parmesan cheese, pepperoni, onion, bell pepper, oregano and garlic.
2. Mix well.
3. Press half of the dough in the bottom and up the sides of a lightly greased deep dish pan.
4. Bake crust in preheated oven for 4 minutes, then add the stuffing mixture to the bottom crust and cover with top crust; seal edges together with fingers, and trim excess.
5. Slit top crust to allow steam to vent during baking; top with tomato sauce.
6. Bake on lower rack at 450 degrees F (230 degrees C) for 45 minutes, or until crust is golden brown.
7. Remove from oven and allow to cool for 5 minutes, then cut and serve.
8. Serve and enjoy!

Chicago Style Pan Pizza

Ingredients:

1 (1 lb.) loaf frozen bread dough, thawed
1 lb. bulk Italian sausage
2 cups shredded mozzarella cheese
8 oz. sliced fresh mushrooms
1 small onion, chopped
2 tsps. olive oil
1 (28 oz.) can diced tomatoes, drained
3/4 tsp. dried oregano
1/2 tsp. salt
1/4 tsp. fennel seed
1/4 tsp. garlic powder
1/2 cup freshly grated Parmesan cheese

Directions:

1. Preheat the oven to 350 degrees F (175 degrees C).
2. Press the dough into the bottom and up the sides of a greased 9x13 inch baking dish.
3. Crumble the sausage into a large skillet over medium-high heat.
4. Cook and stir until evenly browned.
5. Remove the sausage with a slotted spoon, and sprinkle over the dough crust.
6. Sprinkle mozzarella cheese evenly over the sausage.
7. Add mushrooms and onion to the skillet; cook and stir until the onion is tender.
8. Stir in the tomatoes, oregano, salt, fennel seed and garlic powder. Spoon over the mozzarella cheese.
9. Sprinkle Parmesan cheese over the top.
10. Bake for 25 to 35 minutes in the preheated oven, or until crust is golden brown.
11. Serve and enjoy!

Chicago Macaroni Salad

Ingredients:

1 (8 oz.) package salad macaroni
1 cup small broccoli florets
3/4 cup diced Cheddar cheese
1/2 cup chopped green bell pepper
1/2 cup dill pickle relish, with juice
1 large dill pickle, chopped
1/2 cup chopped celery
1/2 cup sliced black olives
1/2 cup sliced green olives (optional)
1/4 cup chopped green onion
2 tbsps. shredded carrot
1 tbsp. chopped pimento peppers
1 cup light mayonnaise
1/4 cup prepared yellow mustard
1 tsp. salt
1/2 tsp. white sugar
1/4 tsp. black pepper

Directions:

1. Fill a pot with lightly salted water and bring to a rolling boil over high heat. Once the water is boiling, stir in the salad macaroni, and return to a boil.
2. Cook the pasta uncovered, stirring occasionally, until the pasta has cooked through, but is still firm to the bite, about 8 minutes.
3. Drain well in a colander set in the sink, and rinse with cold water until chilled.
4. Drain again to remove excess water.
5. Place macaroni, broccoli, Cheddar cheese, green pepper, pickle relish, dill pickle, celery, black olives, green olives, green onion, carrot, and pimento in a salad bowl, and toss lightly to combine.
6. In a bowl, whisk together the light mayonnaise, mustard, salt, sugar, and black pepper to make a smooth dressing; pour the dressing over the salad, and lightly mix to coat all ingredients
7. dressing. Refrigerate at least 4 hours to blend flavors before serving.

8. Serve and enjoy!

Chicago Chili

Ingredients:

2 pounds ground beef
4 (14.5 oz.) cans kidney beans
4 (15 oz.) cans diced tomatoes
1 (12 fl. oz.) bottle beer
1 (12 oz.) bottle tomato-based chili sauce
1 large white onion, chopped
6 cloves garlic, minced 2 tbsps. chili seasoning
1 tsp. black pepper
1/2 tsp. garlic powder
1/2 tsp. onion powder
1/2 tsp. cayenne pepper
1/2 tsp. oregano
1/4 cup sugar 1 tsp. hot sauce
1 tsp. Worcestershire sauce

Directions:

1. Place the ground beef in a large pot and cook over medium heat until evenly brown.
2. Drain off the excess fat.
3. Mix in the kidney beans, diced tomatoes, beer, chili sauce, onion, garlic, chili seasoning, black pepper, garlic powder, onion, cayenne pepper, oregano, sugar, hot sauce, and Worcestershire sauce.
4. Bring to a boil.
5. Reduce heat to low, and simmer for about 4 hours, stirring occasionally.
6. Serve and enjoy!

Chicago Italian Beef Sandwich

Ingredients:

5 lbs rump roast
2 (10 1/4 oz.) cans beef broth
1 (1 oz.) package Italian salad dressing mix
1 jar pepperoncini pepper
1 jar giardiniera
3 sweet green peppers
1 loaf long thin French bread

Directions:

1. Cook first 5 ingredients in a Crockpot on low for 18 hours.
2. Turn over at the 6th and 12th hour interval.
3. At the 17th hour cut sweet green peppers into 1/8 ths lengthwise and cook in water on low heat until soft.
4. Cut bread into 6 inch lengths and slice on the side lengthwise.
5. Pull roast apart with a fork, and using tongs, pile bread with meat and juice.
6. (Do not let juice drain before putting on bread. The juice is half the taste of the sandwich.)
7. Lay strips of green pepper on top of the meat.
8. Serve and enjoy!

Chicago Italian Beef Combo

Ingredients:

1 Chicago Italian Beef Sandwich (see recipe above)
1 Italian sausage

Directions:

1. Place the sausage in a large skillet over medium heat, and brown on all sides.
2. Remove from skillet.
3. Prepare the Chicago Italian Beef Sandwich according to the recipe above, but put the sausage on the French bread before the other ingredients.
4. Add the rest of the Italian Beef Sandwich fixings to the sandwich.
5. Serve and enjoy!

Chicago Chicken Casserole

Ingredients:

4 boneless chicken breasts
1 package chopped broccoli (cook per directions)
1 can corn (drained)
1 can cream of mushroom soup
1/4 cup milk
1/2 lb Velveeta cheese (cut in cubes)
1/2 jar mushroom (more if desired)
1 jar pimiento
Ritz cracker (crumbled)
butter

Directions:

1. Poach chicken in water, when cool enough to handle pull apart into bite-size pieces.
2. In a large 9x12 casserole layer cooked chicken, drained corn and broccoli.
3. Mix soup with milk, cheese, mushrooms and pimentos.
4. Heat and pour over chicken.
5. Sprinkle top with Ritz crackers which have been mixed with enough butter to moisten.
6. If prepared ahead and refrigerate, do not top with the Ritz until ready to bake.
7. Bake for 1 hour or till bubbly and hot.
8. Do not fill casserole to full; this cooks over easily.
9. Serve and enjoy!

Chicago Beer Burger

Ingredients:

1 1/2 lbs. minced beef
2 tbsps. beer
1/2 tsp. Tabasco sauce
1/4 tsp. Worcestershire sauce
4 slices cheese

Directions:

1. Combine beef, beer, Tabasco and Worcestershire sauce.
2. Season to taste.
3. Form into four 1" thick patties.
4. Wrap in cling film and chill for a couple of hours.
5. Grill patties; top with cheese and beer braised onions.
6. Serve and enjoy!

Chicago Chicken Salad

Dressing Ingredients:

1/2 cup mayonnaise
1/4 cup sour cream
1 tbsp. Dijon mustard
1 tsp. sugar
1/4 tsp. salt
1/4 tsp. white pepper
2 1/2 tsps. lemon juice

Salad Ingredients:

1 1/2 cups boneless skinless chicken breasts
1/2 cup celery, finely chopped
2 tbsps. green onions, finely chopped
1/4 cup pecans, toasted and chopped
1/4 cup seedless grapes, halved
lettuce leaf, for serving

Directions:

1. Preheat oven to 450 degrees F.
2. Bake chicken on a foil lined pan for 20 minutes or until chicken is no longer pink inside.
3. Let chicken cool.
4. Cut chicken in to bite sized pieces and then shred it a bit with your fingers.
5. Mix all dressing ingredients together in large bowl.
6. Add chicken, green onion, pecans, and grapes if you are using them.
7. Mix well.
8. Cover and refrigerate for at least 2 hours.
9. Arrange lettuce leaves on plates and top each with a scoop of salad.
10. Serve and enjoy!

Chicago Bears' Style Sub

Ingredients:

1 Italian bread, 12 inches section
2 oz. genoa salami
2 oz. mortadella
2 oz. hot capicola
2 oz. provolone cheese
3 oz. shredded lettuce
1 oz. shaved onion
8 slices tomatoes
Dressing:
3/4 cup Italian dressing
1/2 cup olive oil
1/4 cup red wine vinegar
3 tbsps. dried oregano

Directions:

1. Slice bread horizontally (but not all the way through) and layer with salami, mortadella, hot capicola and Provolone.
2. Top with layers of lettuce, onions and tomato slices.
3. Whisk dressing ingredients together and drizzle as desired over filling.
4. Cut into 4 3-inch pieces.
5. Serve and enjoy!

Chicago Coffee Cake

Ingredients:

1/2 cup margarine
1 (8 oz.) package cream cheese
1 1/4 cups sugar
2 eggs
1 tsp. vanilla extract
1 3/4 cups flour
1 tsp. baking powder
1/2 tsp. baking soda
1/4 cup milk

Topping Ingredients:

1/4 cup sugar
4 tbsps. flour
4 tsps. cinnamon
4 tbsps. margarine

Directions:

1. In large bowl, cream together margarine, cream cheese and sugar until light.
2. Beat in eggs and vanilla.
3. Sift together flour, baking powder and baking soda.
4. Add to creamed mixture alternately with milk, mixing well.
5. Pour into greased and floured 9 by 13 baking pan.
6. For topping, combine sugar, flour, cinnamon and margarine until crumbly.
7. Sprinkle over batter and bake in 350 degree oven 35 to 40 minutes or until toothpick inserted in center comes out clean.
8. Serve and enjoy!

Chicago Creamed Spinach

Ingredients:

1/4 cup unsalted butter
1 small onion, finely chopped
3 tbsps. flour
1 cup milk or 1 cup half-and-half
1 tsp. instant chicken bouillon granules or 1 tsp. bouillon
1/2 tsp. salt
1/4 tsp. freshly grated nutmeg
1/4 tsp. white pepper
2 (10 oz.) packages frozen chopped spinach, thawed

Directions:

1. Melt the butter in a medium skillet.
2. Add the onion; cook over medium heat until tender, 5-6 minutes.
3. Stir in the flour; cook 1 minute, stirring constantly.
4. Whisk in the milk.
5. Cook, stirring often, until mixture comes to a boil and thickens.
6. Stir in the chicken base, salt, nutmeg and pepper.
7. Set aside.
8. Squeeze the thawed spinach to remove as much water as possible.
9. Add the spinach to the cream sauce; mix well.
10. Cook until spinach absorbs some of the sauce, about 5 minutes.
11. Serve and enjoy!

Chicago Strip Steak

Ingredients:

1 tbsp. extra virgin olive oil
1 clove garlic, minced
1/2 tsp. ground cinnamon
1/2 tsp. white sugar
2 tbsps. apricot preserves
2 (1/2 lb.) New York strip steaks, 1" thick
Salt and pepper to taste

Directions:

1. In a shallow glass dish, mix the olive oil, garlic, cinnamon, sugar, and apricot preserves.
2. Mix well, as the preserves tend to stick until warm.
3. With a knife, make several shallow slashes in both sides of the steaks.
4. Sprinkle with salt and pepper.
5. Place steaks in the dish with the sauce, and turn to coat.
6. Cover with plastic wrap, and refrigerate for at least 1 hour.
7. Preheat grill for high heat.
8. Lightly oil the grill grate.
9. Place steaks on the grill, and discard any remaining sauce.
10. Grill steaks 10 minutes, turning occasionally, or to desired doneness.
11. Serve and enjoy!

Chicago Pizza Pot Pie

Ingredients:

1 lb. Italian sausage
1 jar pizza sauce
1 onion, diced
1 clove garlic, minced
mozzarella cheese
1 recipe pizza crust dough, which didn't make it into the picture

Directions:

1. Spray 4-5 inch diameter oven proof bowls with cooking spray. (about 6 bowls)
2. Brown the sausage with onion and garlic.
3. Rinse sausage under hot water to remove the extra grease.
4. In the prepared bowls, layer the cheese, sausage and then sauce.
5. Roll out the pizza dough.
6. Cover each dish with a piece of dough, pinching to seal around the edge.
7. Bake at 450 degrees until they are golden brown.
8. To serve, turn upside down on a plate and run a butter knife around the edge of the crust to loosen it.
9. Lift off the bowl.
10. Serve and enjoy!

Chicago Ribs

Ingredients:

3 lbs baby back ribs (2 racks)
Rub Ingredients:
1 tbsp. mustard powder
1 tbsp. paprika
1 tbsp. dark brown sugar
1 1/2 tsps. garlic powder
1 1/2 tsps. onion powder
1 1/2 tsps. celery salt
1 tsp. cayenne pepper
1/2 tsp. ground allspice
Sauce Ingredients:
1 1/4 cups ketchup
1/4 cup molasses
1/4 cup cider vinegar
1/4 cup water
1/8 tsp. liquid smoke

Directions:

1. Soak 1 cup hickory chips in water for 15 minutes.
2. Using a paring knife, trim membrane off bone-side of racks.
3. Place on a baking sheet.
4. In a bowl, thoroughly combine rub ingredients.
5. Remove 2 tbsps. and set aside for sauce making.
6. Pat ribs dry and sprinkle remaining spice rub over both sides of both racks.
7. Set barbecue grill for indirect heat.
8. Place hickory chips in a disposable aluminum pie plate directly over heat source.
9. Place a second, large aluminum roasting pan to one side of the heat source, and add 2 cups water.
10. Arrange cooking grates over pans.
11. If using gas, turn on burner under wood chips to high, and other burners to medium.
12. Close lid and preheat 15 minutes.
13. Reduce main burner to medium and turn other burners off.
14. Place ribs over pan of water, bone side up.
15. Cook 90 minutes, turning once halfway through.
16. Place a rack over a baking sheet.

17. Pour enough water in bottom to just cover.
18. Transfer ribs to rack and wrap tightly in foil.
19. Place pan in preheated 250 degrees F oven for another 1½-2 hours.
20. Transfer to cutting board, tent with foil and rest 10 minutes.
21. Combine ketchup, molasses, vinegar, water, liquid smoke, and reserved spice rub. Whisk thoroughly.
22. Mop ribs thoroughly with sauce, using about 1 cup of sauce.
23. Serve remaining sauce on the side.
24. Serve and enjoy!

South Side Chicago Barbeque Skirt Steak

Ingredients:

4 lb. trimmed skirt steaks
2 cups olive oil
1 cup red wine
2 tbsps. dried parsley
2 tbsps. dried basil
2 tbsps. balsamic vinegar
2 tbsps. soy sauce
6 cloves garlic, crushed
2 bay leaves
2 cups barbeque sauce

Directions:

1. Make diagonal cuts through the skirt steak on both sides.
2. Cut diagonally about every 1/4 to 1/2 inch, then cut diagonally in the opposite, perpendicular direction.
3. Repeat on the other side of the steak to complete the crisscross cuts that will tenderize the meat. When the meat is prepared, some sections will be very long.
4. I cut the longer sections to keep them under 18 inches long.
5. Whisk together the olive oil, red wine, parsley, basil, balsamic vinegar, soy sauce, garlic, and bay leaves in a large glass or ceramic bowl.
6. Add the skirt steaks and toss to evenly coat.
7. Cover the bowl with plastic wrap, and marinate in the refrigerator for 8 hours to overnight.
8. Preheat an outdoor grill for medium heat, and lightly oil the grate.
9. Remove the skirt steaks from the marinade, and shake off excess. Discard the remaining marinade.
10. Cook the skirt steak on the preheated grill to your desired degree of doneness, about 10 minutes per side for medium-well.
11. Once nearly finished, brush the steaks with the barbeque sauce and cook for 2 minutes.
12. Flip the steaks over, brush with barbeque sauce, and cook 2 minutes longer.

13. Serve and enjoy!

Chicago Deep Dish Pizza Dough

Ingredients:

1 (.25 oz.) package active dry yeast
1/3 cup white sugar
2/3 cup water
2 cups all-purpose flour
1 cup bread flour
1/4 cup corn oil
2 tsps. salt
6 tbsps. vegetable oil
1/2 cup all-purpose flour, or as needed

Directions:

1. Dissolve yeast and sugar in water in a bowl.
2. Let stand until the yeast softens and begins to form a creamy foam, about 5 minutes.
3. Mix 2 cups all-purpose flour, bread flour, corn oil, and salt together in a bowl.
4. Add yeast mixture and knead on a work surface using about 1/2 all-purpose flour until well mixed.
5. Let dough rise in a warm area until doubled in size, about 2 hours.
6. Serve and enjoy!

Chicago Shrimp DeJonghe

Ingredients:

2 cups dry white wine
1 cup butter, melted
2 cloves garlic, minced
1 pinch ground cayenne pepper
1/2 tsp. paprika
1 cup chopped fresh parsley
2 cups fresh bread crumbs

Directions:

1. Preheat oven to 350 degrees F (175 degrees C).
2. Lightly grease an 11x 7" casserole dish.
3. Place shrimp evenly in the casserole dish.
4. Pour wine over the shrimp.
5. Mix together butter, garlic, cayenne pepper, paprika, parsley and bread crumbs.
6. Sprinkle bread crumb mixture over the shrimp.
7. Refrigerate now if desired.
8. Bake in preheated oven for 20 minutes, or until shrimp are firm and topping is golden brown.
9. Serve and enjoy!

Chicago Chicken Vesuvio

Ingredients:

6 medium new potatoes, quartered
4 (6 oz.) skinless, boneless chicken breast halves
2 tsps. olive oil
1/4 cup fresh lemon juice
2 tsps. fresh rosemary, minced
1 tsp. minced garlic salt and pepper to taste
1/8 cup green onions, chopped
1/8 cup pitted black olives, sliced
1/2 cup mushrooms, sliced

Directions:

1. Place potatoes and chicken in a casserole dish.
2. Drizzle with olive oil and lemon juice. Then sprinkle with rosemary, garlic, salt, and pepper.
3. Cover, and refrigerate for at least 30 minutes.
4. Preheat oven to 400 degrees F (200 degrees C).
5. Sprinkle green onions over chicken.
6. Bake, covered, in preheated oven for 30 minutes.
7. Remove, and add olives and mushrooms.
8. Return to oven, and bake for 30 minutes.
9. Transfer chicken and vegetables to platter, and pour pan juices on top.
10. Serve and enjoy!

Chicago Francheezie Hot Dog

Ingredients:

Jumbo Hot Dog
American Cheese or spread cheese (ex: Cheez Whiz)
Bacon
Hot Dog Bun
Condiments of choice

Directions:

1. Slice a jumbo hot dog end to end to make a cheese reservoir. Do not cut all the way through the bottom or all the way to the ends of the hot dog or the cheese will leak out.
2. Fill with as much cheese as you can.
3. Wrap 3 pieces of bacon around the dog.
4. Wrap it as much as you can to stop the cheese from leaking out.
5. Best if deep fried but it can also be grilled.
6. If using a pan, fry it as if you are frying bacon.
7. Toast the hot dog bun if you like on the grill.
8. Top with condiments of your choice.
9. Serve and enjoy!

Chicago Jibarito

Authentic Puerto Rican sandwich with no bread involved!

Ingredients:

1 green plantain, peeled and halved lengthwise
2 tbsps. vegetable oil
1 clove garlic, minced
4 oz. beef skirt steak, cut into thin strips
1/4 medium yellow onion, thinly sliced
1 pinch cumin
1 pinch dried oregano
1 tbsp. mayonnaise
1 slice processed American cheese, cut in half
2 slices tomato
3 leaves lettuce

Directions:

1. Heat 2 cups vegetable oil in a large, deep skillet or deep fryer to 350 degrees F.
2. Place plantain halves in the oil and cook 1 to 2 minutes, until they float.
3. Remove from oil and drain on paper towels.
4. Place plantain halves between 2 cutting boards.
5. Press to flatten.
6. Place the flattened plantains back in the oil and cook for 2-3 minutes, until golden brown.
7. Drain on paper towels.
8. Heat 2 tbsps. of oil in a large skillet.
9. Add the garlic, skirt steak, onion, cumin and oregano.
10. Cook, stirring frequently, until steak is cooked through.
11. To serve, spread mayonnaise on one of the plantain slices.
12. Top with cheese, steak and onion mixture, lettuce, and tomato.
13. Place the other plantain half on top to form a sandwich.
14. Cut in half and serve!
15. Serve and enjoy!

Leroy Brown's Chicago Mother-In-Law

Ingredients:

4 cups Chili (recipe below), or your favorite prepared chili
4 Chicago-style hot tamales (or 4 prepared pork, chicken or beef tamales)
12 sport peppers, chopped
1/4 white onion, chopped
4 hot dog buns
1 1/2 cups shredded Manchego
2 small bags corn chips, such as Fritos, crushed

Chili Ingredients:

1 tsp. vegetable oil
1 1/2 pounds ground sirloin
1 lb. Mexican-style chorizo
1 onion, diced
1 to 2 tbsps. chili powder
1 to 2 tbsps. ground cumin
1 tsp. paprika
Kosher salt and freshly ground black pepper
1 stout beer
1 tbsp. hot sauce
1 (14.5-oz.) can crushed tomatoes

Directions:

1. Heat the Chili ingredients in a small saucepot until it is simmering, about 5 minutes.
2. Prepare the tamales according to package directions.
3. In a small bowl, combine the sport peppers and chopped onion.
4. Place some onions and sport peppers along the bottom of the hotdog buns.
5. Remove the husks of the tamales.
6. Place the tamales in the buns and top with the Manchego.
7. Prepare the chili.
8. In a large Dutch oven, heat the oil over medium heat.
9. Add the beef and chorizo and smoosh down.

10. Start breaking up the chunks with a wooden spoon and let sear until the beef is no longer pink, about 5 minutes.
11. Remove the meat from the pot and leave the fat. Then add the onions, chili powder, cumin, paprika and season with salt and pepper.
12. Cook until the onions are soft, 7 to 8 minutes.
13. Deglaze with the beer
14. Cook until the alcohol smell subsides, 3 to 4 minutes.
15. Add the hot sauce, tomatoes, stock and the reserved meat.
16. Simmer until thickened, stirring frequently, about 20 minutes.
17. Adjust seasoning.
18. Ladle a small amount of chili on top of the tamale on the bun.
19. Top with the remaining sport peppers and onions and sprinkle with the corn chips.
20. Serve and enjoy!

Chicago Popcorn

Chicago Carmel Popcorn Ingredient:

2/3 cup unpopped popcorn
2 tbsps. oil (for popping)
1 cup butter
2 cups brown sugar
1 tsp. salt
1/2 cup corn syrup
1 tsp. baking soda

Directions:

1. Preheat the oven to 200 degrees F.
2. Spray your largest cookie sheets.
3. Pop the popcorn in the oil and set aside. I do this in two batches.
4. Place in a very large bowl. (Plastic bowls work really well because the caramel won't stick; you could also spray the bowl with a bit of Pam).
5. Over medium heat in a heavy saucepan, melt butter and stir in brown sugar, salt and syrup.
6. Bring to a rolling boil.
7. When it starts to boil, boil a full 5 minutes stirring constantly with a wooden spoon. (I used a plastic spatula and ended up sacrificing it)
8. Remove from the heat and add the soda.
9. Pour caramel directly on the popcorn and stir to coat completely.
10. Pour popcorn onto the sheets and bake for 1 hour, stirring every 15-20 minutes. Allow to cool and break into pieces. Store in zip-top bags.

Cheese Popcorn Ingredients:

3 tbsps. melted butter
1/4 cup cheddar cheese powder, plus 1 tbsp.
1/4 tsp. mustard powder
1/4 tsp. cayenne pepper
4 cups popped popcorn
Salt and pepper

Directions:

1. In a large bowl, combine the butter, cheddar cheese powder, mustard powder, cayenne pepper and the popcorn.
2. Season with salt and pepper, to taste and toss to combine. Serve immediately.

3. After making both the Carmel Popcorn recipes and the Cheese Popcorn recipes, mix them together.
4. Serve and enjoy!

Flaming Saganaki

Ingredients:

1 lb kasseri cheese, sliced 1/2-inch thick
2 tbsps. olive oil, more if needed
1/4 cup all-purpose flour
1/2 cup brandy or 1/2 cup ouzo
2 fresh lemons, cut into wedges
4 pita bread, warmed and cut into triangles for serving

Directions:

1. Slice the cheese into 1/2" thick triangles or 3-4" squares
2. Place brandy into a zip-lock baggie and add cheese portions, seal and let marinate for 2 hours.
3. Heat oil in a cast iron skillet over a med/high heat.
4. Remove cheese portions from marinade, reserving marinade for later use.
5. Dredge cheese thru the flour, shaking off excess.
6. Fry the cheese slices approx. 2 minutes, flip with spatula and fry an additional 1-2 minutes.
7. Remove from heat when nicely seared on each side and gooey.
8. Pour 1 oz. of the brandy marinade over the top of the fried cheese, and immediately set ablaze with a lighter.
9. Yell "Opa!" and immediately squeeze a lemon slice over the top to dowse the flames.
10. Serve with warmed pita slices and additional lemon wedges.
11. Serve and enjoy!

Chicago Pizza Puff

Tortilla Ingredients:

2 cups of all-purpose flour
1/2 tsp. salt
1 tsp. baking powder
1 tbsp. lard
3/4 cup warm water

Filling Ingredients:

8 oz. cooked and crumbled mild sausage
6 oz. tomato paste
2 tbsps. fennel seed
1/4 cup mozzarella cheese

Tortilla Directions:

1. Combine the dry ingredients
2. Cut in the lard
3. Add water all at once and mix with your hands, kneading as you go
4. To make a dough that holds together well as a ball.
5. 4Roll out onto a floured surface.
6. 5Use the Pocket Maker to cut out circles.
7. This recipe made about 16 circles for me - enough for 8 pizza puffs.
8. 1After you have cooked the sausage, save about a tbsp. of the fat from the pan and put the sausage into a food processor.
9. 2Add in the other ingredients and pulse until mixture resembles a paste.
10. If too crumbly, add in the tbsp. of sausage grease to better hold it together
11. Assembly
12. Add about a tbsp. of filling to half of the circles that you cut out and use an egg wash to make the top circle stick.
13. Grab the Pocket Maker again and place on top of your circles, pressing the button on top.
14. Lift and check out the cool little seal it put on!
15. I put these in the deep fryer (350°) for about 5 minutes, flipping once, or until they were golden brown.
16. Serve and enjoy!

Chicago Atomic Cake

Ingredients:

1 layer banana or yellow cake shopping list
1 layer chocolate cake
1 layer white cake
Fresh bananas, sliced
1 small box Jell-O banana Pudding
fresh strawberries, sliced
Grated chocolate
1 small box Jell-O chocolate pudding
1 small box Jell-O vanilla Pudding
whipped cream

Directions:

1. Set the banana (or yellow) cake layer on a cake plate.
2. Top with sliced bananas, then spread banana pudding over the top to hold the bananas together.
3. Spread whipped cream over pudding.
4. Place the chocolate cake layer on top.
5. Sprinkle with grated chocolate.
6. Top with sliced strawberries, then spread chocolate pudding over the top.
7. Spread with whipped cream.
8. Place the white cake layer on top.
9. Spread with vanilla pudding.
10. Frost top of cake with a generous amount of whipped cream.
11. Refrigerate.
12. Serve and enjoy!

Chicago Greek Gyro

Ingredients:

1/2 onion, cut into chunks
1 lb. ground lamb
1 lb. ground beef
1 tbsp. minced garlic
1 tsp. dried oregano
1 tsp. ground cumin
1 tsp. dried marjoram
1 tsp. ground dried rosemary
1 tsp. ground dried thyme
1 tsp. ground black pepper

Directions:

1. Place the onion in a food processor, and process until finely chopped.
2. Scoop the onions onto the center of a towel, gather up the ends of the towel, and squeeze out the liquid from the onions.
3. Place the onions into a mixing bowl along with the lamb and beef.
4. Season with the garlic, oregano, cumin, marjoram, rosemary, thyme, black pepper, and salt.
5. Mix well with your hands until well combined.
6. Cover, and refrigerate 1 to 2 hours to allow the flavors to blend.
7. Preheat oven to 325 degrees F (165 degrees C).
8. Place the meat mixture into the food processor, and pulse for about a minute until finely chopped and the mixture feels tacky.
9. Pack the meat mixture into a 7x4 inch loaf pan, making sure there are no air pockets. Line a roasting pan with a damp kitchen towel.
10. Place the loaf pan on the towel, inside the roasting pan, and place into the preheated oven.
11. Fill the roasting pan with boiling water to reach halfway up the sides of the loaf pan.
12. Bake until the gyro meat is no longer pink in the center, and the internal temperature registers 165 degrees F (75 degrees C) on a meat thermometer, 45 minutes to 1 hour.

13. Pour off any accumulated fat, and allow to cool slightly before slicing thinly and serving with cucumber sauce.
14. Serve and enjoy!

Cucumber Sauce

Ingredients:

6 tbsps. sour cream
1 tbsp. mayonnaise
1/2 tsp. garlic powder
1/2 tbsp. lemon juice
1/2 tsp. dried dill (optional)
1 large cucumber (seeded, peeled and chopped or grated)
1 pinch salt (to taste)
1 pinch pepper (to taste)

Directions:

1. Put the cucumber into a colander and sprinkle with a little salt.
2. Let rest for 10-15 minutes to allow extra juices to escape the cucumber.
3. Gently squeeze the cucumber in a paper or cloth towel.
4. Put everything a bowl and mix well.
5. Add salt and pepper to taste.
6. Refrigerate for a couple of hours prior to using.
7. A turn or two in the food processor would yield a nice smooth sauce.
8. Serve and enjoy!

Maxwell Street Polish Sausage Sandwich

Ingredients:

1 tbsp. vegetable oil
4 links Polish kielbasa sausage, patted dry with a paper towel
(about 1 1/2 pounds)
1 yellow onion, thinly sliced
Kosher salt and freshly ground black pepper
4 fresh poppy seed hot dog buns
Yellow mustard
6 to 10 pickled sport peppers

Directions:

1. Preheat the oven to 175 degrees F.
2. Heat the oil over medium heat in a heavy-bottomed skillet.
3. Add the sausages and cook on each side, undisturbed, until golden brown, about 5 minutes a side. Set on a baking dish in the oven to keep warm.
4. To the same skillet, add the onions and stir to combine with the oil.
5. Season the onions with salt and pepper and cook over medium-low heat, undisturbed, until the bottom of the onions begin to caramelize, about 10 minutes.
6. Stir only once and cook for another 25 minutes, undisturbed.
7. Once the onions are golden and soft, set aside.
8. Place a sausage on a bun, slather in yellow mustard, top with an ample amount of caramelized onions and 2 or 3 sport peppers.
9. Wrap the sandwich in deli paper, parchment paper or foil.
10. Let sit for 5 minutes.
11. Serve and enjoy!

Chicago Breaded Steak Sandwich

Ingredients:

4 flank steaks, sliced thin
Flour for dredging
2 eggs
1/4 cup of milk
1 cup Italian seasoned bread crumbs
4 tbsps. of fresh grated Parmesan cheese
1/2 tsp. salt
1/2 tsp. fresh ground black pepper
4 tbsps. of vegetable oil
1 tbsps. butter
Marinara sauce, heated
Italian dinner rolls
1/2 cup of mozzarella cheese, shredded

Directions:

1. Dip the steaks in the flour then pound out thin. (about 1/4 inch)
2. In a wide container mix together the eggs and milk
3. In another dish, mix together the bread crumbs, Parmesan cheese, salt and pepper.
4. Heat the oil and butter in a large skillet.
5. Dip the steaks into the egg and then the breadcrumb mixture.
6. Fry the steaks in the oil and butter on both sides until golden brown.
7. Place the steaks on a paper towel covered plate to drain.
8. Dip the steaks in the hot marinara and place on the bread.
9. Top with shredded mozzarella,
10. Add sweet peppers and/or hot or mild giardinaira.
11. Serve and enjoy!

Pullman Loaf

Ingredients:

1 1/2 cups lukewarm water
1 cup (5 1/2 oz.) semolina flour
2 tbsps. honey
2 1/4 tsps. instant yeast
2 cups (9 oz.) bread flour
1/2 cup white wheat flour
1 1/2 tsps. salt
3 tbsps. butter

Directions:

1. In the bowl of your stand mixer, combine the water, semolina flour, honey, yeast, and bread flour.
2. Stir to combine.
3. Cover and set aside for 20 minutes.
4. Add the white wheat flour, salt, and butter and knead with the dough hook attachment of your stand mixer until the dough is smooth and elastic. Flour your work surface lightly, and knead by hand briefly, then form the dough into a ball. Drizzle with olive oil and return it to the bowl.
5. Cover with plastic wrap and set aside for 30 minutes.
6. Preheat the oven to 350 degrees. turn out the dough and knead it briefly to knock out the large bubbles.
7. Form it into a log about 13 inches long - to fit inside the pan.
8. Place the log in the pan, seam-side down.
9. Put the lid on the pan and set aside until the dough has risen to within about an inch of the top of the pan - about 40 minute (but you might want to check at 30 minutes, just in case)
10. Bake at 350 degrees until the loaf is golden brown, about 40 minutes.
11. Remove the loaf from the pan and allow it to cool completely on a rack before slicing.

Palmer House Brownies

Brownie Ingredients:

1 lb. plus 2 oz. semi-sweet chocolate
1 lb. butter
12 oz. granulated sugar
8 oz. cake flour
1 Tbsp baking powder
4 large whole eggs
1 lb crushed, toasted walnuts

Apricot Glaze Ingredients:

1 cup water
1 cup apricot preserves
1 envelope unflavored gelatin powder

Directions:

1. Make brownies: Melt chocolate with butter in a double boiler or heat-proof bowl suspended over very hot water.
2. Mix dry ingredients in a mixing bowl (except walnuts.) Mix melted chocolate/butter mixture with dry ingredients.
3. Whisk in eggs, one at a time, taking about 5 minutes continuous whisking from the first egg to the last. Butter and flour a 9 x 12 baking dish.
4. Preheat oven to 350. Toast walnuts for about 15 minutes until fragrant. Lower oven temperature to 300. Chop walnuts and set aside.
5. Spread brownie batter into the prepared pan. It will be very liquid.
6. Sprinkle surface with the chopped walnuts, pressing down so that they are partly submerged.
7. Bake in 300 degree oven 45 to 50 minutes until the brownies have crisped on the edge of the pan–about 2-inches around the full edge of the pan. The brownies in the center of the pan will remain slightly jiggly. Note: even when properly baked, these brownies will test "gooey" in the center with a toothpick test, due to the richness of the batter.

8. Remove brownies from oven and cool on a rack for 30 minutes. Chef Stephen Henry says for cleanest slices, freeze the brownies for three hours after glazing. Then cut, and serve while very firm and cold.
9. Make glaze: Mix water, preserves and unflavored gelatin in a saucepan over medium heat.
10. Whisk until boiling; heat at boiling for two minutes. While the glaze is still hot, spread a thick layer over the brownies. Cool completely.
11. Place in the freezer for 3 to 4 hours.
12. Slice and serve while very cold and firm.

Chicago Hot Dog-Style Salmon

Ingredients:

cooking spray
4 (6 oz.) salmon fillets
1/4 lemon, juiced, or more to taste
2 tsps. dried dill weed
1/4 cup Dijon mustard
2 large dill pickles, diced
1/2 white onion, diced
1 tomato, seeded and diced
4 sport peppers, chopped, or to taste (optional)
1 dash celery seed, or to taste

Directions:

1. Preheat oven to 400 degrees F (200 degrees C).
2. Spray four 6x6-inch pieces of aluminum foil with cooking spray.
3. Place salmon fillets on top.
4. Drizzle lemon juice over salmon fillets; sprinkle 1/2 tsp. of dill weed over each one.
5. Spread 1 tbsp. mustard onto each salmon fillet; top with dill pickle and onion.
6. Wrap aluminum foil around salmon, sealing the edges.
7. Place packets onto a baking sheet.
8. Bake in preheated oven until fish flakes easily with a fork, about 15 minutes.
9. Place packets in shallow bowls; open with heatproof gloves. Top with diced tomatoes and sport peppers; season with celery seed.

Chicago Fish Soup

Ingredients:

1 med. onion, chopped
2 cloves garlic, finely minced
1/2 cup thinly sliced celery
3 tbsp. butter
1 (29 oz.) can tomatoes, coarsely chopped
1 cup diced potatoes
1 (12 oz.) can or bottle beer
1 tsp. dried crushed basil
1 tsp. dried crushed oregano
1 tsp. salt
1 dash of pepper
1/4 tsp. crushed dried red peppers
1 cup fresh corn kernels
1/2 lb. salmon steaks, boned and cut into cubes
1/4 lb. whitefish, cubed or 1/2 lb. whitefish and omit the smelt
1/4 lb. smelt, boned and cubed

Directions:

1. Saute onions, garlic, green pepper and celery in butter in a large saucepot or Dutch oven until tender, about 15 minutes.
2. Add tomatoes, potatoes and beer.
3. Add basil, oregano, salt, pepper and red peppers. Simmer until potatoes are almost tender, about 15 minutes.
4. Add corn and fish, continue simmering about 10 minutes or until fish is done.

Chicago Lasagna

Ingredients:

1 onion chopped
1 lb. ground turkey or buffalo
2 cans chopped tomatoes
2 cans tomato sauce
12 lasagna noodles, cooked
1 tsp. basil
2 tsp. oregano
1 lb. mozzarella cheese, sliced
Parmesan cheese

Directions:

1. Sauté onion with ground meat until meat is browned.
2. Drain any grease.
3. Add tomatoes, sauce, basil and oregano. Simmer 20 minutes.
4. In 9 x 13 inch pan, place 4 noodles.
5. Sprinkle with parmesan cheese, layer with 1/3 of mozarella cheese. Ladle 1/3 sauce over cheese.
6. Repeat 2 times with remaining ingredients.
7. Bake at 350 degrees F until hot and bubbly for about 45 minutes.

Chicago Buttermilk Cake

Ingredients:

1 box white cake mix (no pudding)
1 sm. box instant vanilla pudding
1 sm. box instant lemon pudding
5 eggs
1/2 cup water
1/2 cup vegetable oil
1/2 cup sweet milk

Topping Ingredients:

1 stick butter
1 cup sugar
1/2 tsp. baking soda
1/2 cup buttermilk

Directions:

1. Preheat oven to 300 degrees F.
2. Mix all Cake ingredients together well.
3. Pour into a bundt pan sprayed with cooking spray.
4. Bake for about 1 hour.

Topping Directions:

5. Melt butter and sugar together in a sauce pan.
6. Add baking soda and butter.
7. Slowly heat to a boil.
8. Boil 1 minute.
9. Pour over warm cake while sauce is hot.

Chicago Chicken With Rice

Ingredients:

Bread crumbs
1 egg, beaten
Wild rice
1 block of cheddar cheese (like Cracker Barrel)
1 pound chicken breasts cut into strips
Vegetable oil for frying

Directions:

1. Wrap chicken around small chunk of cheese.
2. Secure with toothpicks.
3. Dip in egg, then bread crumbs.
4. Heat vegetable oil in a pan.
5. Brown prepared chicken in heated pan.
6. Drain on paper towels.
7. Prepare wild rice and spread in Pyrex pie dish.
8. Arrange chicken rolls on top of the rice.
9. Bake at 350 degrees F for 30 minutes.
10. Serve and enjoy.

Black Hawk Creamed Spinach (Chicago)

Ingredients:

1 (#2 1/2 can) spinach, strain juice
3 slices bacon
1 sm. onion, minced
1 1/2 tsp. flour
Salt and pepper to taste

Directions:

1. Fry bacon, add 1 small onion and brown in grease.
2. Add 1 1/2 tsps. flour to make the thickening.
3. Add the spinach juice and cook until smooth, then add chopped spinach.
4. Cook 5 to 10 minutes until spinach has mixed thoroughly. Crumble bacon pieces and spread on top of spinach.

Chicago Crunchy Chocolate Chip Cookies

Ingredients:

1 cup butter
1 cup sugar
1 cup brown sugar
1 egg
1 tbsp. milk
2 tsps. vanilla extract
3 1/2 cups all-purpose flour
1 tsp. salt
3 tsps. baking powder
1 cup vegetable oil
1 cup oats, quick cooking
1 cup corn flakes
12 oz. chocolate chips

Directions:

1. Cream butter with sugars. Add egg, milk and vanilla. Combine flour, salt and baking powder.
2. Add these dry ingredients alternately with oil to the first mixture. Add oats, corn flakes and chocolate chips.
3. Drop by teaspoonful onto ungreased cookie sheets.
4. Bake at 350 degrees (180 degrees C) for 10 to 13 minutes.
5. Makes about 8 dozen cookies.

Chicago Chicken

Ingredients:

6-8 chicken breasts
1 lg. can whole cranberries, not jellied
1 pkg. onion soup mix
1 bottle Russian salad dressing (with honey)
Cooked rice for serving

Directions:

1. Place chicken in a baking dish.
2. Mix together cranberries, onion soup mix, and salad dressing.
3. Pour over chicken.
4. Bake 1 hour, covered at 350 degrees.
5. Bake 15 minutes uncovered.
6. Serve with rice.

Chicago Goulash

If you're not from Chicago, you may want to add tomato sauce.

Ingredients:

1 package elbow macaroni
1 pound hamburger
1/4 cup chopped onion
1/2 tsp. salt

Directions:

1. Cook macaroni according to package directions.
2. Drain well.
3. Brown the hamburger in a skillet with the onion.
4. Drain if necessary.
5. Add hamburger and onion to cooked macaroni with the salt.
6. Mix well and serve.
7. This is Chicago style.
8. If not from Chicago, you may want to add tomato sauce.

Chicago Fudge Cake

Ingredients:

1/2 cup butter
2 cup brown sugar, packed
2 egg yolks
1 tsp. vanilla
4 squares baking chocolate
1/2 cup hot water
2 1/2 cup sifted cake flour
1 tsp. baking soda
1/2 tsp. salt
1/2 cup sour milk
2 egg whites
1/4 tsp. cinnamon
1/2 cup raisins
1/4 cup chopped nutmeats

Directions:

1. Cream the butter and brown sugar and add the egg yolks and vanilla; beat well.
2. Melt the chocolate over simmering water and add to the creamed mixture. Rinse the chocolate pan with the hot water and add to the chocolate and creamed mixture.
3. Then beat in the flour, sifted with the baking soda and salt, alternately with the sour milk.
4. Beat the egg whites until stiff and fold into the chocolate batter. (Reserve 1 1/2 cups batter for the third layer pan.)
5. Pour remaining batter into 2 greased and floured 8" layer pans.
6. Stir the cinnamon, raisins and nuts into the reserved batter and pour into a greased and floured 8" layer pan.
7. Bake all in a moderate oven, 350 degrees, for about 30 minutes or until done. When baked and cooled, ice the cake all over with fluffy vanilla icing.
8. Put the layer with the raisins, nuts and cinnamon in the middle. and before frosting is dry, sprinkle with milk chocolate bar; finely grated.

Chicago Hot Relish

Ingredients:

8 lb. ripe tomatoes, don't peel, chop and drain 1/2 day
2 cup chopped celery
6 big onions, chopped
6 red and 6 green mangoes, chopped
2 tbsp. mustard seed
2 tbsp. cinnamon
2 tbsp. sugar
1/2 cup salt
1 qt. vinegar (scant)

Directions:

1. Mix cold. Don't cook.
2. Add hot peppers if you like. Don't seal. Refrigerate.
3. Makes 1 1/2 gallon.
4. Excellent in BBQ, goulash, cheese balls, potato salad about anything mixed up or hamburgers, along side any meat.

Chicago Hot Relish

Ingredients:

1 peck ripe tomatoes, chopped fine
6 med. onions, chopped
4 green bell peppers, chopped
4 red bell peppers, chopped
2 lg. stalks celery, chopped
4 hot peppers, chopped
2 cup horseradish, ground
3 cup sugar
4 cup vinegar
3 tbsp. mustard seed
3 tbsp. celery seed
1/2 cup salt

Directions:

1. Combine chopped tomatoes, onions, peppers, celery and horseradish.
2. Mix well.
3. Sprinkle salt over vegetables and mix thoroughly. Put in a muslin bag and let drain overnight.
4. Add sugar and spices to vinegar; simmer 15 minutes.
5. Add vegetables and heat to boiling. Pack, boiling hot, into hot pint jars. Process 10 minutes in boiling water bath.

Chicago Hot Sauce

Ingredients:

2 gallons tomatoes, chopped
4 cup chopped onions
2 cup chopped green peppers
2 cup chopped hot peppers
2 cup chopped celery
1 qt. vinegar
1/2 cup salt
2 cup sugar
1/3 cup white mustard seed

Directions:

1. Mix all ingredients together and store in refrigerator.
2. Do not seal as it will not be the same if it's cooked and sealed.
3. Just cover and keep it in the refrigerator instead.

Chicago Stew

Ingredients:

1 1/2 - 2 lbs. beef (lamb or pork)
2 twists of pepper mill
5 potatoes (quarters or sixths)
Fresh parsley
1 or 2 white turnips
1 cup tomatoes
1 tsp. salt (less is preferred)
1 lg. or 2 sm. onions
6 carrots
1 can peas (not baby peas) or green beans or corn or all 3
Meat (cut chunk size)

Directions:

1. Trim all fat and gristle and put in pan for browning. Brown meat in bacon drippings or butter.
2. Use a Dutch oven with cover. Each piece of meat is wiped with a damp cloth and rolled in flour. Brown meat. When browned, add enough hot water to cover meat.
3. Cover and simmer gently - beef- 1 1/2 to 2 hours; pork 45 minutes to one hour.
4. Prepare vegetables. Keep in cold water until all ready.
5. All vegetables can be cooked (except potatoes) together as soon as prepared.
6. Add potatoes 20 minutes after the vegetables start cooking.
7. Add only enough water to cover vegetables.
8. When meat is done, remove meat to platter. Thicken au jus with flour for gravy.
9. Keep adding a little liquid from vegetables.
10. Stir until thickened.
11. Add vegetable liquid until gravy is the thickness you desire. Return meat to gravy. Strain rest of vegetable liquid and save in freezer for other gravies.
12. Add vegetables to meat and gravy, or you can keep gravy and meat together and vegetables separate.

Chicago Pita Pizzas

Ingredients:

2 baby eggplants (4 oz. each)
2 green onions
1/4 tsp. salt
2 cup shredded Mozzarella cheese (8 oz.)
Fresh basil for garnish
1/4 lb. mushrooms
3 tbsp. olive or salad oil
4 (6") pitas
3/4 cup pizza sauce
2 tbsp. grated Parmesan cheese

Directions:

1. Cut the eggplants into 1/2" chunks Cut each mushroom into quarters.
2. Cut green onions into 1" pieces.
3. Preheat oven to 450 degrees. In 10" skillet over medium-high heat, in hot oil, cook eggplant, mushrooms, green onions and salt, stirring frequently, until lightly browned and tender, about 5 minutes.
4. Remove skillet from heat.
5. Cut small slit on one side of each pita; fill with Mozzarella cheese.
6. Place pitas on cookie sheet.
7. Spread pizza sauce over pitas. Top with vegetables; sprinkle with Parmesan cheese.
8. Bake 5 to 7 minutes until cheese melts. Garnish with basil.

Chicago Cake

Ingredients:

1 cup Crisco shortening
2 cup granulated sugar
5 lg. or extra lg. eggs
1 cup milk
3 cup flour
3 tsp. baking powder
1/4 tsp. salt
1 tsp. vanilla

Directions:

1. Cream together shortening and sugar.
2. Add eggs, one at a time.
3. Add milk and flour and beat well.
4. Combine remaining ingredients and add.
5. Bake at 350 degrees for 1 hour in angel food pan with Pam or shortening and flour.

Chicago Baked Beans

Ingredients:

1 lb. ground beef
1/4 cup brown sugar
1/2 lb. bacon, cut up
1/2 cup chopped onion
3 tbsp. vinegar
2 tbsp. mustard
1 can baked beans
1 can kidney beans
1 can butter beans

Directions:

1. Saute ground beef, cut up bacon, and onion (drain fat from mixture). Add remaining ingredients.
2. Put in casserole dish and bake 1 1/2 hours at 325 degrees. Stir several times while baking.

Chicago Style Spinach Pizza

Ingredients:

1 can (10 oz.) refrigerated pizza crust
1 pkg. (10 oz.) chopped spinach, thawed, well drained
1 pkg. (16 oz.) part-skim mozzarella cheese, shredded
1/4 cup (1 oz.) Parmesan cheese, shredded, divided
1 can (28 oz.) tomatoes, drained, cut up
2 garlic cloves, minced
2 tsp. dried oregano leaves
1/2 tsp. red pepper flakes, optional

Directions:

1. Heat oven to 500 degrees F. Press pizza crust onto bottom and sides of well greased 10 inch deep dish pizza pan or 9 x 13 inch baking dish.
2. Mix spinach, mozzarella cheese and 2 tbsps. Parmesan.
3. Spread evenly over crust.
4. Mix tomatoes, garlic, oregano and pepper flakes.
5. Spread over cheese mixture.
6. Sprinkle with remaining 2 tbsps. Parmesan cheese.
7. Bake 10 minutes.
8. Reduce heat to 375 degrees and bake for an additional 20 minutes.

Chicago Public School Cafeteria Butter Cookies

Ingredients:

1 cup unsalted butter, softened
2/3 powdered sugar
2 tsps. vanilla extract
2 cups flour, plus
2 tbsps. flour

Directions:

1. Preheat over to 350 degrees F.
2. Cream butter and powdered sugar until fluffy.
3. Add vanilla extract.
4. Mix in flour in small increments.
5. Roll dough into balls; flatten on ungreased cookie sheets.
6. Bake until golden brown around the edges.

Oh My Spaghetti Pie

Alfredo Pie Ingredients:

1/4 cup unsalted butter
1/4 cup all purpose flour
2 cups whole milk
1 cup heavy cream
Pinch ground nutmeg
2 cups Italian Five Cheese blend shredded cheese, divided
3/4 cup grated Parmesan cheese, divided
Salt and pepper, to taste
12 oz. spaghetti

Marinara Ingredients:

2 (28 oz.) cans whole tomatoes, packed in juice
2 tbsps. olive oil
1 medium onion, chopped fine (about 1 cup)
2 medium cloves garlic, minced or pressed through garlic press (about 2 tsps.)
1/2 tsp. dried oregano
1/3 cup dry red wine such as Cabernet Sauvignon or Merlot
3 tbsps. chopped fresh basil
1 tbsp. extra virgin olive oil
Salt and ground black pepper
1 - 2 tsps. sugar, as needed
Fresh basil, chopped, for topping
Equipment:
1 (9 1/2-10-inch) deep dish pie plate, sprayed with non-stick spray

Directions:

1. Adjust an oven rack to the middle position and preheat oven to 350 degrees F.
2. Remove 1/2 cup shredded Italian five cheese from the bag, and add to a small bowl mixing it with 1/4 cup shredded Parmesan, set aside for topping the partially baked pie.
3. Combine heavy cream and milk in one measuring cup.
4. Melt butter in a medium saucepan over medium heat until foaming, whisk in flour until combined, continue whisking until mixture is smooth and slightly golden, about 1 minute.

5. Gradually add milk and heavy cream, increase heat to medium-high and whisk constantly to combine into a
6. Once sauce is thickened, start adding the cheese, a handful at a time, stirring after each addition waiting until the cheese is melted before adding more.
7. Continue adding, and stirring, until the 2 cups of cheese is melted and the sauce is smooth.
8. Taste and add salt and pepper as needed, you may only need some pepper since the cheese is somewhat salty.
9. Turn heat off but leave pan on burner, cover, and keep warm until ready to toss with spaghetti.
10. Cook pasta and begin baking pie while marinara cooks.
11. Pour tomatoes and juice into strainer set over large bowl. Open tomatoes with hands and remove and discard fibrous cores; let
12. tomatoes drain excess liquid, about 5 minutes.
13. Remove 3/4 cup tomatoes from strainer and set aside.
14. Reserve 2 1/2 cups tomato juice and discard remainder.
15. Heat olive oil in large skillet over medium heat until shimmering.
16. Add onion and cook, stirring occasionally, until softened and golden around edges, 6 to 8 minutes.
17. Add garlic and oregano and cook, stirring constantly, until garlic is fragrant, about 30 seconds.
18. Add tomatoes from strainer and increase heat to medium-high.
19. Cook, stirring every minute, until liquid has evaporated and
20. tomatoes begin to stick to bottom of pan and brown fond forms around pan edges, 10 to 12 minutes.
21. Add wine and cook until thick
22. and syrupy, about 1 minute.
23. Add reserved tomato juice and bring to simmer; reduce heat to medium and cook, stirring occasionally and loosening browned bits, until sauce is thick, 8 to 10 minutes.
24. Transfer sauce to food processor (or transfer to saucepan and insert immersion blender; and add reserved tomatoes; process until slightly chunky, about eight 2-second pulses (you can make it as thick or as smooth as you like).
25. Return sauce to skillet and add basil and extra-virgin olive oil and salt, pepper, and sugar to taste.
26. Bring a large pot of water to boil over high heat.

27. Add 1 tbsp. salt then spaghetti, stirring occasionally to separate the strands.
28. Cook until al dente (even slightly firmer than al dente since it will soften more as it bakes).
29. Drain the pasta and return to the pot.
30. Stir the Alfredo sauce again to make sure it's smooth, then add all but 1 cup to the spaghetti and toss to combine.
31. Return the cover to the Alfredo and keep it warm (my oven has a warming burner, if you don't, warm it gently over low heat before topping the partially baked pie with it.)
32. If you feel the sauce is too thick and not coating all of the pasta easily you can add some of the pasta cooking water, a little at a time, until the sauce is thoroughly mixed with the pasta.
33. Transfer the spaghetti to the pie dish and pat down the top to make an even layer.
34. Bake for 20 minutes.
35. Re-stir the Alfredo sauce so it's once again smooth.
36. Top the pie with the remaining Alfredo sauce.
37. Sprinkle the remaining 3/4 cup cheese on top of the Alfredo sauce, return to oven for 10 minutes, or until cheese is melted and light golden brown.
38. Rotate your baking sheet front to back halfway through baking.
39. Remove from oven and let pie rest 10 minutes.
40. Spread a layer of marinara sauce on each serving plate, or shallow bowl, cut pie into pieces and serve on top of marinara.
41. Sprinkle with fresh basil.
42. Serve and enjoy!

About the Author

Laura Sommers is **The Recipe Lady!**

She is a loving wife and mother who lives on a small farm in Baltimore County, Maryland and has a passion for all things domestic especially when it comes to saving money. She has a profitable eBay business and is a couponing addict. Follow her tips and tricks to learn how to make delicious meals on a budget, save money or to learn the latest life hack!

Visit her Amazon Author Page to see her latest books:

amazon.com/author/laurasommers

Visit the Recipe Lady's blog for even more great recipes:

http://the-recipe-lady.blogspot.com/

Follow the Recipe Lady on **Pinterest**:

http://pinterest.com/therecipelady1

Follow her on Facebook:

https://www.facebook.com/therecipegirl/

Please leave a review:

It's proven that generosity makes you a happier person. So if you are generous enough to leave me a review for this cookbook, then thank you. It has really helped me and my family a lot. I hope that this book has enriched your life.

Other Books by Laura Sommers

Irish Recipes for St. Patrick's Day

Traditional Vermont Recipes

Traditional Memphis Recipes

Maryland Chesapeake Bay Blue Crab Cookbook